P9-DOD-902

INDIGENOUS PEOPLES' DAY

by Katrina M. Phillips

PEBBLE
a capstone imprint

Pebble Explore is published by Pebble, an imprint of Capstone.
1710 Roe Crest Drive
North Mankato, Minnesota 56003
capstonepub.com

Library of Congress Cataloging-in-Publication Data is available on the Library of Congress website.
ISBN: 9781663926401 (hardcover)
ISBN: 9781663926340 (paperback)
ISBN: 9781663926357 (ebook PDF)

Summary: Indigenous Peoples' Day is about celebrating! The second Monday in October is a day to honor Native American people, their histories, and cultures. People mark the day with marches, dancing, and food. Readers will discover how a shared holiday can have multiple traditions and be celebrated in all sorts of ways.

Image Credits
Alamy: Jeffrey Isaac Greenberg 9+, 20, Pat Canova, 8, SCPhotos, 24; Associated Press: Elaine Thompson, 5, 12, Marty Lederhandler, 29, Ted S. Warren, 18; Getty Images: Boston Globe, 27, San Francisco Chronicle/Hearst Newspapers via Getty Images, 26; Library of Congress, 11; Newscom: Danita Delimont Photography/David R. Frazier, 14, Danita Delimont Photography/Luc Novovitch, 15, Reuters/Arnd Wiegmann, 22, Reuters/Deanna Dent, 23, Reuters/Eduardo Munoz, 1, 17, ZUMA Press/Paul Christian Gordon, 7, 19; Shutterstock: HannaTor, Cover, The Old Major, 25

Artistic elements: Shutterstock: Rafal Kulik

Editorial Credits
Editor: Erika L. Shores; Designer: Dina Her; Media Researcher: Jo Miller; Production Specialist: Tori Abraham

All internet sites appearing in back matter were available and accurate when this book was sent to press.

TABLE OF CONTENTS

Words in **bold** are in the glossary.

WHAT IS INDIGENOUS PEOPLES' DAY?

Some holidays are old. Others are not. But new holidays can teach us a lot. Indigenous Peoples' Day started in 1992. It is the second Monday in October. Indigenous means to be the very first to live in a place.

Indigenous Peoples' Day celebrates Native Americans in the United States. More people celebrate Indigenous Peoples' Day every year. In some places, the day is called Native American Day. Lots of cities and states celebrate Indigenous Peoples' Day. Does yours?

On Indigenous Peoples' Day, people think about the past. It is a time to remember the promises the U.S. government has made to Native Americans. The government has made **treaties**, or agreements, with Native people for many years.

People want to honor Native American culture. Culture is the way of life for a group of people. It is the language, art, music, and traditions. The holiday shows pride in the things Native people have done.

About 6 million Native people live in the United States. Their **ancestors** have lived here for thousands of years. They were here long before Europeans arrived.

There are hundreds of Native nations in the United States. Native people live all across the United States. They live in big cities. They live in small towns. They may live on **reservations**. Or they might not. Which Native nations are in your state?

CHANGING THE STORY

Indigenous Peoples' Day is the same day as Columbus Day. Columbus Day has been a U.S. holiday since 1934. But many Native and Indigenous people do not want to celebrate Christopher Columbus.

Christopher Columbus did not discover North America. There were already lots of people here! Columbus kidnapped Indigenous people. He **enslaved** many of them. Because of this, people do not want to celebrate him.

Christopher Columbus

Drummers sing as they lead a march on Indigenous Peoples' Day.

People who celebrate Indigenous Peoples' Day want to celebrate and learn about all the things Native people have done. They want to honor people like the **Taíno**. They were the first people Columbus met. Many people who live on islands in the Caribbean have Taíno ancestors.

A TIME TO GATHER

People celebrate Indigenous Peoples' Day in many ways. They may cook some traditional foods. They might cook wild rice or make **fry bread**.

Making fry bread

People may go see Elders. They hear stories about the past. Others may visit other Native leaders. They talk about the things that are important to people in their communities.

Some Native people go to a **powwow** to celebrate. If they do, they might wear **regalia**. This clothing is worn for special events.

Native communities may gather for a feast. They might host a powwow. There could be dancers and drum groups. They may hold ceremonies and parades.

In the state of Minnesota, many people gather at the Minneapolis American Indian Center. They gather for food and dancing. They see family and friends. It is one of the oldest Indian centers in the country.

The United Indians of All Tribes Foundation hosts **rallies** and marches. This group is in Seattle, Washington. They celebrate the work which led the city to recognize Indigenous Peoples' Day.

Native people in the area celebrate with traditional songs and dances. They also have a traditional salmon dinner. They gather at the Daybreak Star Indian Cultural Center in Seattle.

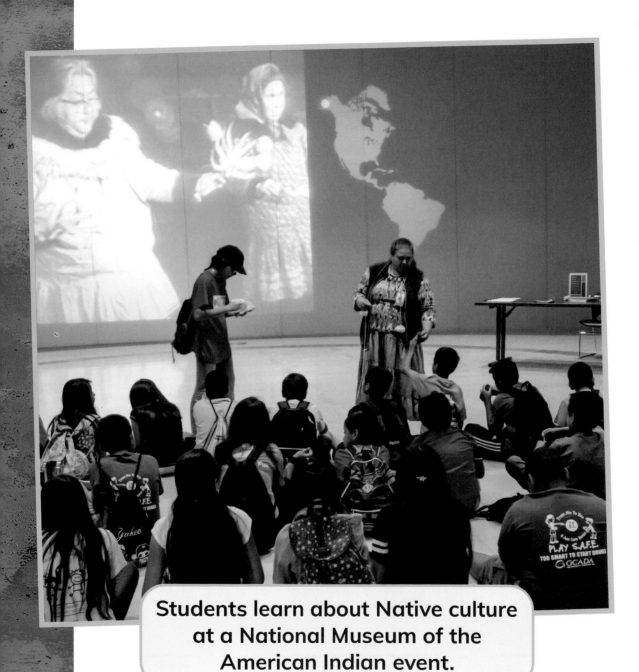

Students learn about Native culture at a National Museum of the American Indian event.

Indigenous Peoples' Day is a way to celebrate Native art and culture. Some people celebrate by reading poems. In 2020, three Native poets, Sherwin Bitsui, Joan Naviyuk Kane, and Tommy Pico, read their poems for an event in Brooklyn, New York.

People go to museums. The National Museum of the American Indian in Washington, D.C., has art on display by Native painters. There might be singers or drum groups there. Native authors may share their books. People might give speeches. They remember their ancestors.

Some people think Native people have disappeared. But that is not true. Native people are still here. Native people have a long history of **activism**. Many people wanted a day to celebrate and learn.

You could learn about Autumn Peltier. She is a water protector. Water protectors are people who want to keep water safe and clean. Peltier has spoken out for clean water her whole life.

Autumn Peltier

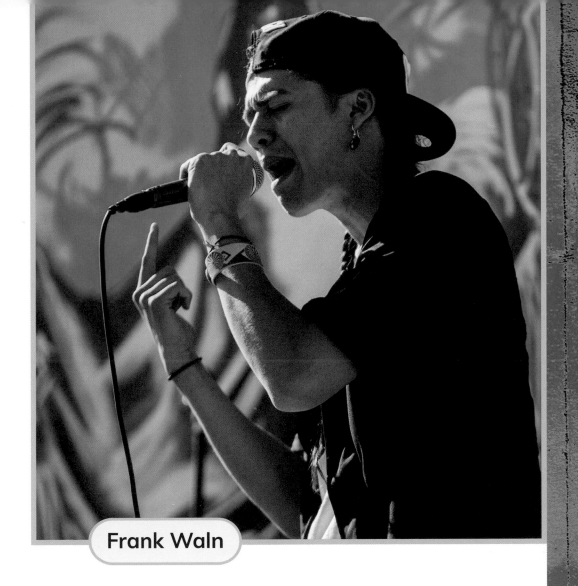

Frank Waln

You could also learn about Frank Waln. He is an activist and a hip hop artist. He wrote a song to let people know about a project that would harm Native lands.

MORE THAN A DAY

Indigenous Peoples' Day is just one day. Native people celebrate their past all year. They honor their cultures all year. They learn their languages. They teach their languages. They practice traditional ceremonies.

Every summer Native nations in the Pacific Northwest go on the Tribal Canoe Journey. They travel the same water routes as Native people long ago. They build canoes to travel along the West Coast. Canoes are an important part of their culture. The Tribal Canoe Journeys are a time for many nations to gather and celebrate.

Indigenous people in the United States hold two big events in November. The Indigenous Peoples' Sunrise Ceremony is also called Un-thanksgiving Day. It is the fourth Thursday of November. It began in 1975. It is held in San Francisco Bay in California.

People dancing at the Sunrise Ceremony

Fire and smoke stand for healing during a National Day of Mourning ceremony.

The Native Americans of New England host the National Day of Mourning. It is also on the fourth Thursday in November. These events remind people about things that matter to Native peoples.

AROUND THE WORLD

August 9 is the International Day of the World's Indigenous People. The day brings attention to the needs of Indigenous people all over the world. More than 370 million Indigenous people live across more than 90 countries. There are many ways to celebrate Indigenous people!

A ceremony in New York City honored the first International Day of the World's Indigenous People in 1995.

GLOSSARY

activism (AK-tiv-uh-ism)—to bring about political or social change

ancestor (AN-sess-tur)—a family member who lived a long time ago

enslave (en-SLAYV)—to force someone to lose their freedom

fry bread (FRYE BRED)—a flat dough bread that can be fried or deep fried, made with simple ingredients; not a "traditional" Native food, but many Native nations made it when they did not have their traditional foods on reservations

powwow (POW-wow)—a social gathering where Native people sing, dance, and honor their cultures

rally (RAL-lee)—an event that brings people together to get ready for action

regalia (ruh-GEI-lee-uh)—what Native dancers wear for special occasions

reservation (rez-er-VAY-shuhn)—an area of land set aside for Native people

Taíno (TYE-no)—an indigenous people of the Caribbean; some Puerto Ricans, Cubans, and Dominicans still identify as Taíno

treaty (TREE-tee)—an agreement between two or more nations

READ MORE

Keene, Adrienne. *Notable Native People: 50 Indigenous Leaders, Dreamers, and Changemakers from Past and Present*. Emeryville, CA: Ten Speed Press, 2021.

Rice, Dona Herweck. *American Indian Leaders Today*. Huntington Beach, CA: TCM, Teacher Created Materials, 2021.

Sorell, Traci. *We Are Still Here!: Native American Truths Everyone Should Know*. Watertown, MA: Charlesbridge, 2021.

INTERNET SITES

Map: Making Indigenous Peoples Day Official Across the Country
indiancountrytoday.com/news/map-making-indigenous-peoples-day-official-across-the-country

National Museum of the American Indian: Americans
americanindian.si.edu/americans/

National Park Service: Indigenous Heritage
nps.gov/subjects/tellingallamericansstories/indigenousheritage.htm

INDEX